STICK & LEARN
Brrm!

THINGS *that go*

TOP THAT

Licensed exclusively to Top That Publishing Ltd
Tide Mill Way, Woodbridge, Suffolk, IP12 1AP, UK
www.topthatpublishing.com
Copyright © 2017 Tide Mill Media

Chugga-chug!

The big **red tractor** has **work** to do,

but it needs some **wheels!**

Find a **big** wheel and a **small** wheel. **Stick** them on the tractor so it can plough the **fields.**

Chugga-chug!

Chugga-chug!

tractor

small

big

Tractors do different jobs like **ploughing** fields and **sowing** seeds.

Find the sticker!

Hoot!

The enormous **container** ship

sails across the sea with its **cargo.**

Find more **colourful** **containers** and **stick** them on the **ship.**

Hoot!
Hoot!
Hoot!

ship

containers

The containers are full of **food, cars** and **clothes** that are ready to be **delivered.**

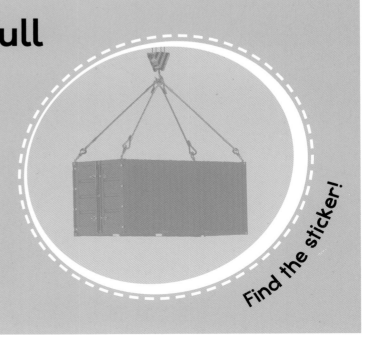

Find the sticker!

Choo!

The **train** is whizzing **along the tracks,**

out of the **tunnel.**

Find **two train carriages** and **stick** them on the **tracks.**

Choo! Choo! Choo!

train

tracks

Some trains move **people**, others move **heavy cargo.** That's **hard work!**

Find the sticker!

Whoosh!

The **aeroplane** is coming in to land.

It's been a
long flight!

Find another
aeroplane and
stick it in the **sky.**

It's next to land!

Whoosh! Whoosh! Whoosh!

sky

aeroplane

Big aeroplanes can carry over **500** people! Prepare for **take-off!**

Find the sticker!

Digga-dig!

The **digger** is hard at work,

but it needs a **bucket** to **dig** the earth.

Find a **bucket** and **stick** it on the **digger** so it can get the **job done!**

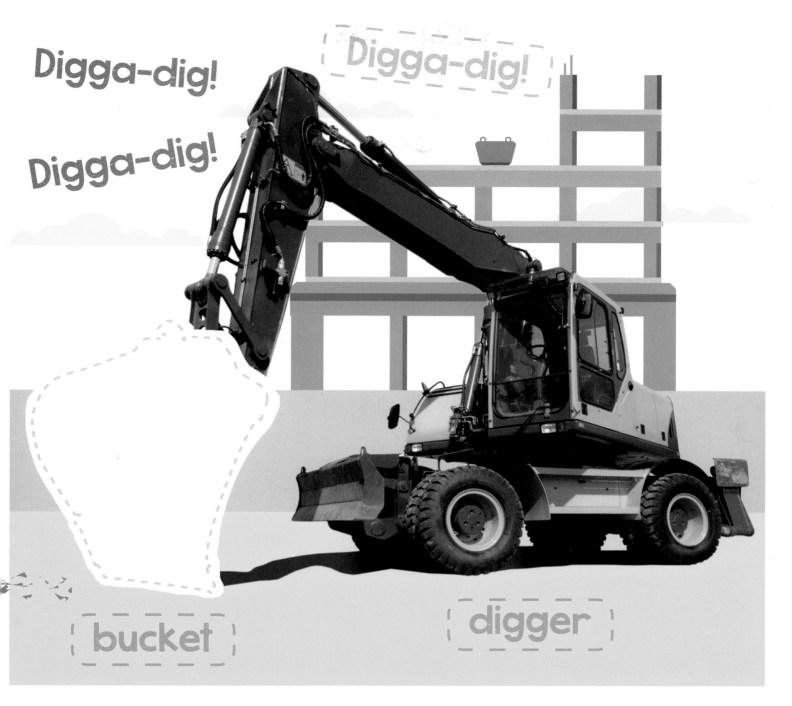

Digga-dig!

Digga-dig!

Digga-dig!

bucket

digger

This **little digger** is perfect for working in **small spaces.** Good work, digger!

Find the sticker!

Rumble!

The **dumper truck** is really big. See how it **dumps** its heavy load.

It is **moving** lots of sand.

Find the dumper truck's **heavy load** and **stick** it on the **ground**.

Rumble!
Rumble!

Rumble!

sand   dumper truck

This is one of the biggest dumper trucks in the world! **It's enormous!**

Find the sticker!

Zoom!

The **rocket** is leaving **Earth** to travel into **space**.

It is very, very **fast!**

Find some **flames** and **stick** them **under** the **rocket!**

Zoom! Zoom! Zoom!

space

rocket

Earth

Rockets take **astronauts** to the **Space Station,** high above Earth.

Find the sticker!

Woomph!

The **hot-air balloon** is being filled with hot air.

It's going **higher and higher!**

Find **two hot-air balloons** and **stick** them in the **sky**.

Woomph! Woomph! Woomph!

sky

hot-air balloon

It can be very **quiet** in a hot-air balloon. **Shh** ... don't disturb the animals!

Find the sticker!

Vroom!

Look at the **racing car** go!

It is **very noisy** and **very fast!**

Find **two more racing cars** and **stick** them on the **track.**

Vroom! Vroom! Vroom!

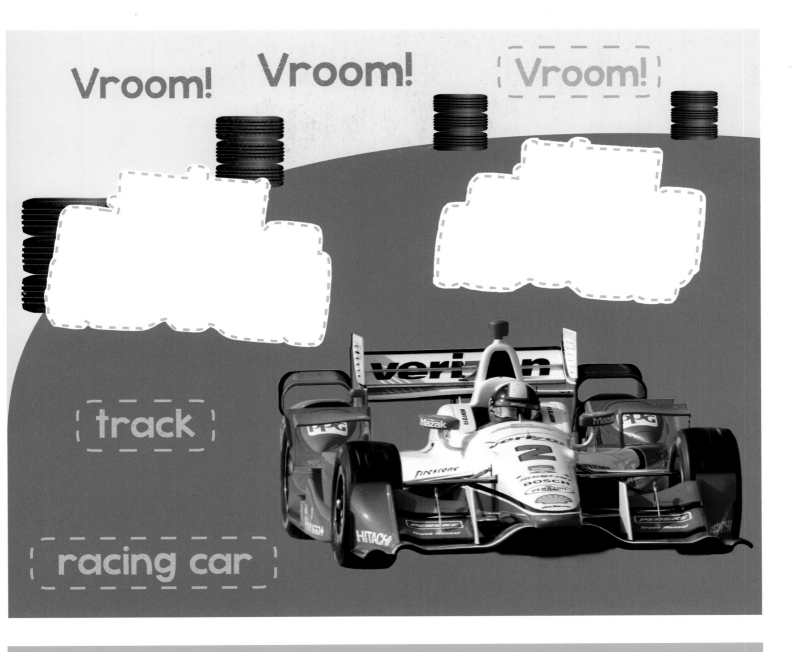

track

racing car

Racing car **drivers** always wear a **helmet** to keep them safe. 3 ... 2 ... 1 ... Go!

Find the sticker!

Flap!

The **sailing boat** is powered by the **wind**.

It needs **sails** to make it **go!**

Find **two more sails** and **stick** them on the **sailing boat** to catch more wind.

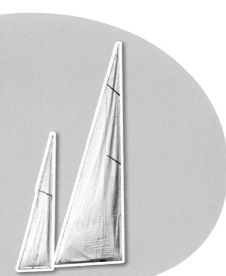

Flap!

Flap!

Splash!

sail

boat

This boy is learning to **sail** in a little boat. It is lots of **fun!**

Find the sticker!

Brrm!

The **motorbike** is **speeding** around the corner.

What an **exciting** race!

Find **three more motorbikes** and **stick** them where they can join in the **race!**

Brrm! Brrm! Brrm!

motorbike

Some motorbikes are perfect for muddy **bumps and jumps!** Hold on!

Find the sticker!

Thwack-thwack!

The **helicopter** is taking off.

Thwack-thwack!

helicopter

Find another helicopter and **stick** it in the **sky.**

Chugga-chug!

tractor

big

small

Hoot!

Choo!

tracks

train

Whoosh!

aeroplane

Digga-dig!

digger

bucket

Rumble!

sand

dumper truck

Zoom!   **space**   **rocket**

Earth

Woomph!

Vroom!

hot-air balloon

sky

racing car

track

Flap!

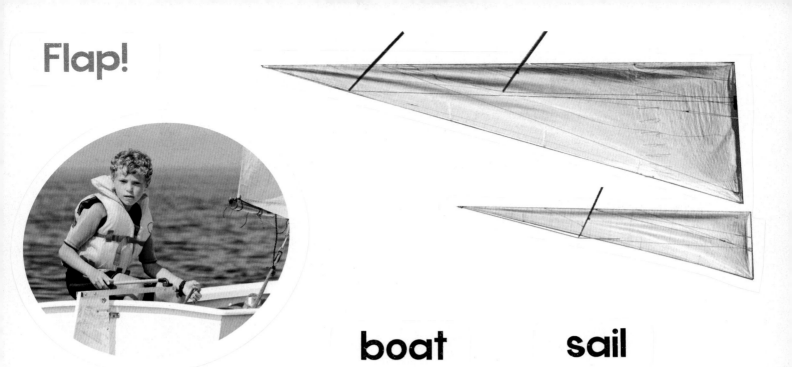

boat   **sail**

Brrm!

motorbike

Thwack-thwack!

helicopter

Use these stickers in this book.

Use these stickers anywhere you like.

Use these stickers anywhere you like.